Communicative Language Teaching:

- Origins
- Fundamentals
- Applications

Lutfiya Esanova

© Esanova Lutfiya
**Communicative Language Teaching:
Origins, Fundamentals, Applications**
By: Esanova Lutfiya
Edition: June '2024
Publisher:
Taemeer Publications LLC (Michigan, USA / Hyderabad, India)

ISBN 978-93-5872-984-9

© Esanova Lutfiya

Book	:	Communicative Language Teaching: Origins, Fundamentals, Applications
Author	:	Esanova Lutfiya
Publisher	:	Taemeer Publications
Year	:	'2024
Pages	:	82
Title Design	:	*Taemeer Web Design*

CONTENTS

FOREWORD 7

CHAPTER I. INTRODUCTION TO COMMUNICATIVE LANGUAGE TEACHING 9

    What is Communicative Language Teaching? 9

    The Goal of Language Teaching 10

        Communicative competence 10

    How Learners Learn a Language 11

    The Kinds of Classroom Activities That Best Facilitate Learning 12

    The Roles of Teachers and Learners in the Classroom 13

CHAPTER II. THE DEVELOPMENT STAGES OF COMMUNICATIVE LANGUAGE TEACHING .. 14

    Phase 1: Traditional Approaches (up to the late 1960s) 14

    Phase 2: Classic Communicative Language Teaching (1970s to 1990s) 17

    Proposals for Communicative Syllabus 19

        Skills-based syllabus 19

        Functional syllabus 20

    English for Specific Purposes 21

    Implications for Methodology 23

CHAPTER III. FUNDAMENTALS OF COMMUNICATIVE LANGUAGE TEACHING 24

    Fundamental 1. Communication as the Goal 25

        Theoretical Foundations 25

        Empirical Evidence 25

        Practical Implications 25

        Model Lesson Plan 1 26

        Model Lesson Plan 2 27

        Model Lesson Plan 3 27

        Model Lesson Plan 4 28

    Fundamental 2. Authentic Language Use 29

        Theoretical Foundations 29

        Empirical Evidence 29

        Practical Implications 29

        Model Lesson Plan 1 30

        Model Lesson Plan 2 31

Fundamental 3. Real-Life Contexts 32

    Theoretical Foundations: 32

    Empirical Evidence: 32

    Practical Implications 32

    Model Lesson Plan 1: 33

    Model Lesson Plan 2 34

Fundamental 4. Task-Based Learning 35

    Theoretical Foundations 35

    Empirical Evidence: 35

    Practical Implications 35

    Model Lesson Plan 1 36

    Model Lesson Plan 2 37

Fundamental 5. Student-Centered Approach 38

    Theoretical Foundations: 38

    Empirical Evidence: 38

    Practical Implications 38

    Model Lesson Plan 1 39

    Model Lesson Plan 2 40

Fundamental 6. Contextual Learning 41

    Theoretical Foundations: 41

    Empirical Evidence: 41

    Practical Implications 41

    Model Lesson Plan 1 42

    Model Lesson Plan 2 43

Fundamental 7. Language Functions over Structures 44

    Theoretical Foundations 44

    Empirical Evidence Insights 44

    Practical Implications 44

    Model Lesson Plan 1 45

    Model Lesson Plan 2 46

Fundamental 8. Cultural Sensitivity 47

    Theoretical Foundations 47

    Empirical Insights 47

    Practical Implications 47

    Model Lesson Plan 1 48

    Model Lesson Plan 2 49

Fundamental 9. Error Tolerance 50

    Theoretical Foundations: 50

    Empirical Insights: 50

    Practical Implications 50

    Model Lesson Plan 1 51

    Model Lesson Plan 2 52

Fundamental 10. Interactive Communication 53

    Theoretical Frameworks: 53

    Practical Applications: 53

    Practical Implications: 53

    Model Lesson Plan 1 54

    Model Lesson Plan 2 55

Fundamental 11. Use of Technology 56

    Theoretical Foundations 56

    Practical Strategies 56

    Practical Implications 56

    Model Lesson Plan 1 57

    Model Lesson Plan 2 58

Fundamental 12. Assessment Through Performance 59

    Theoretical Foundations: 59

    Practical Applications: 59

    Practical Implications: 59

    Model Lesson Plan 1 60

    Model Lesson Plan 2 61

CHAPTER IV. CURRENT TRENDS IN COMMUNICATIVE LANGUAGE TEACHING 62

  Ten Core Assumptions in Modern CLT 62

  Essential Characteristics of Traditional Classroom Activities 63

  Key Components of CLT in Today's World 64

  Eight Major Changes in Approaches to Language Teaching 65

CHAPTER V. CLASSROOM ACTIVITIES IN CLT 68

  Fluency & Accuracy Practices 68

    Fluency Tasks 69

    Accuracy Tasks 69

  Mechanical, Meaningful, and Communicative Practice 71

    Sample Exercise from CLT Coursebook 72

  Information-Gap Activities 73

  Jigsaw activities 74

  Other Activity Types in CLT 74

FOREWORD

    Task-completion activities 75

    Information-gathering activities 75

    Opinion-sharing activities 75

    Information-transfer activities 75

    Reasoning-gap activities 75

    Role plays 75

    Language Games 76

    Problem-Solving Activities: 76

  Emphasis on Pair and Group Work 76

  The Push for Authenticity 77

Conclusion 79

FOREWORD

Welcome to our first work "**Communicative Language Teaching: Origins, Fundamentals, and Current Trends**", a comprehensive manual that navigates the intricate landscape of Communicative Language Teaching (CLT). Rooted in theoretical foundations, this manual aims to unravel the historical origins, delve into the fundamental principles, and explore the current trends that shape this transformative approach to language education. In this manual, we will examine the methodology known as commu- nicative language teaching, or CLT, and explore the assumptions it is based on, its origins and evolution since it was first proposed in the 1970s, and how it has influenced approaches to language teaching today. Since its inception in the 1970s, CLT has served as a major source of influence on language teaching practice around the world.

As language teaching paradigms evolved, CLT emerged as a groundbreaking methodology that prioritizes communication as the core objective. This manual serves as a guide for educators, learners, and language enthusiasts seeking a nuanced understanding of CLT—from its inception to its contemporary applications. Theoretical foundations form the bedrock of any pedagogical approach, and CLT is no exception. This manual delves into the theoretical underpinnings that shaped the birth of CLT, drawing on key concepts such as communicative competence, socio-cultural theories, and task-based language teaching. Understanding these foundations provides a lens through which we can appreciate the rationale behind the fundamental principles of CLT. The fundamentals of CLT encapsulate a range of principles, from prioritizing communication over rote memorization to fostering a learner-centered environment. Each fundamental aspect, whether it be the focus on language functions, real-life contexts, or the integration of technology, contributes to the overarching goal of preparing learners for authentic language use.

In recognition of the dynamic nature of language education, this manual explores current trends within CLT. From the integration of technology to the emphasis on cultural sensitivity and the utilization of performance-based assessments, the manual navigates the contemporary landscape, providing insights into how CLT continues to evolve in response to the challenges and opportunities presented by the digital age.

FOREWORD

Through model lesson plans and practical examples, this manual bridges theory and practice. Whether you are an experienced educator looking to refine your instructional strategies or a learner seeking to understand the principles guiding your language education, "CLT: Origins, Fundamentals, and Current Trends" offers a comprehensive journey through the transformative realm of Communicative Language Teaching. Many of the issues raised by a communicative teaching methodology are still relevant today, though teachers who are relatively new to the profession may not be familiar with them. This manual therefore serves to review what we have learned from CLT and what its relevance is today. Let this manual be your companion in unlocking the richness of CLT, paving the way for effective and engaging language learning experiences.

Author

CHAPTER I. INTRODUCTION TO COMMUNICATIVE LANGUAGE TEACHING

What is Communicative Language Teaching?

Perhaps the majority of language teachers today, when asked to identify the methodology they employ in their classrooms, mention "communicative" as the methodology of choice. However, when pressed to give a detailed account of what they mean by "communicative," explanations vary widely. In our opinion, Communicative language teaching can be understood as a set of principles about the goals of language teaching, how learners learn a language, the kinds of classroom activities that best facilitate learning, and the roles of teachers and learners in the classroom. We will examine each of these issues in turn. Before we begin, let us check your understanding about Communicative Language Teaching:

Your turn:
Which of the statements below do you think characterizes communicative language teaching, and why you think so?

1. People learn a language best when using it to do things rather than through studying how language works and practicing rules.

2. Grammar is no longer important in language teaching.

3. People learn a language through communicating in it.

4. Errors are not important in speaking a language.

5. CLT is only concerned with teaching speaking.

6. Classroom activities should be meaningful and involve real communication.

7. Dialogs are not used in CLT.

8. Both accuracy and fluency are goals in CLT.

9. CLT is usually described as a method of teaching.

_____
_____
_____
_____
_____

CHAPTER I. INTRODUCTION TO COMMUNICATIVE LANGUAGE TEACHING

The Goal of Language Teaching

Communicative language teaching sets as its goal the teaching of *communicative competence*. What does this term mean? Perhaps we can clarify this term by first comparing it with the concept of *grammatical competence*. Grammatical competence refers to the knowledge we have of a language that accounts for our ability to produce sentences in a language. It refers to knowledge of the building blocks of sentences (e.g., parts of speech, tenses, phrases, clauses, sentence patterns) and how sentences are formed. Grammatical competence is the focus of many grammar practice books, which typically present a rule of gram- mar on one page, and provide exercises to practice using the rule on the other page. The unit of analysis and practice is typically the sentence. While gram- matical competence is an important dimension of language learning, it is clearly not all that is involved in learning a language since one can master the rules of sentence formation in a language and still not be very successful at being able to use the language for meaningful communication. It is the latter capacity which is understood by the term communicative competence.

Communicative competence

Communicative competence includes the following aspects of lan- guage knowledge:
- Knowing how to use language for a range of different purposes and functions
- Knowing how to vary our use of language according to the setting and the participants (e.g., knowing when to use formal and informal speech or when to use language appropriately for written as opposed to spoken communication)
- Knowing how to produce and understand different types of texts (e.g., narratives, reports, interviews, conversations)
- Knowing how to maintain communication despite having limitations in one's language knowledge (e.g., through using different kinds of communication strategies)

Your turn:

Consider the following sentences that are all requests for someone to open a door. Imagine that the context is normal communication between two friends. Check if you think they conform to the rules of grammatical competence (GC), communicative competence (CC), or both.

	GC	CC
Please to opens door.		
I want the door to be opened by you.		
Would you be so terribly kind as to open the door for me?		
Could you open the door?		
To opening the door for me.		
Would you mind opening the door?		
The opening of the door is what I request.		

How Learners Learn a Language

Our understanding of the processes of second language learning has changed considerably in the last 30 years and CLT is partly a response to these changes in understanding. Earlier views of language learning focused primarily on the mastery of grammatical competence. Language learning was viewed as a process of mechanical habit formation. Good habits are formed by having students produce correct sentences and not through making mistakes. Errors were to be avoided through controlled opportunities for production (either written or spoken). By memorizing dialogs and performing drills, the chances of making mistakes were minimized. Learning was very much seen as under the control of the teacher.

In recent years, language learning has been viewed from a very different perspective. It is seen as resulting from processes such as:

- Interaction between the learner and users of the language
- Collaborative creation of meaning
- Creating meaningful and purposeful interaction through language
- Negotiation of meaning as the learner and his or her interlocutor arrive at understanding
- Learning through attending to the feedback learners get when they use the language
- Paying attention to the language one hears (the input) and trying to incorporate new forms into one's developing communicative competence
- Trying out and experimenting with different ways of saying things

The Kinds of Classroom Activities That Best Facilitate Learning

With CLT began a movement away from traditional lesson formats where the focus was on mastery of different items of grammar and practice through con- trolled activities such as memorization of dialogs and drills, and toward the use of pair work activities, role plays, group work activities and project work.

Your turn:

Examine a classroom text, either a speaking text or a general English course book. Can you find examples of exercises that practice grammatical competence and those that practice communicative competence? Which kinds of activities predominate?

The Roles of Teachers and Learners in the Classroom

The type of classroom activities proposed in CLT also implied new roles in the classroom for teachers and learners. Learners now had to participate in classroom activities that were based on a cooperative rather than individualistic approach to learning. Students had to become comfortable with listening to their peers in group work or pair work tasks, rather than relying on the teacher for a model. They were expected to take on a greater degree of responsibility for their own learning. And teachers now had to assume the role of facilitator and monitor. Rather than being a model for correct speech and writing and one with the primary responsibility of making students produce plenty of error-free sentences, the teacher had to develop a different view of learners' errors and of her/his own role in facilitating language learning.

Your turn:
What difficulties might students and teachers face because of changes in their roles in using a communicative methodology?

_____
_____
_____
_____
_____
_____
_____
_____
_____
_____
_____

CHAPTER II. THE DEVELOPMENT STAGES OF COMMUNICATIVE LANGUAGE TEACHING

In planning a language course, decisions have to be made about the content of the course, including decisions about what vocabulary and grammar to teach at the beginning, intermediate, and advanced levels, and which skills and microskills to teach and in what sequence. Decisions about these issues belong to the field of **syllabus design** or **course design**. Decisions about how best to teach the contents of a syllabus belong to the field of **methodology**.

Language teaching has seen many changes in ideas about syllabus design and methodology in the last 50 years, and CLT prompted a rethinking of approaches to syllabus design and methodology. We may conveniently group trends in language teaching in the last 50 years into three phases:

Phase 1: traditional approaches (up to the late 1960s)
Phase 2: classic communicative language teaching (1970s to 1990s)
Phase 3: current communicative language teaching (late 1990s to the present)

Let us first consider the transition from traditional approaches to what we can refer to as classic communicative language teaching.

Phase 1: Traditional Approaches (up to the late 1960s)

As we saw in Chapter 1, traditional approaches to language teaching gave priority to grammatical competence as the basis of language proficiency. They were based on the belief that grammar could be learned through direct instruction and through a methodology that made much use of repetitive practice and drilling. The approach to the teaching of grammar was a *deductive* one: students are presented with grammar rules and then given opportunities to practice using them, as opposed to an *inductive* approach in which students are given examples of sentences containing a grammar rule and asked to work out the rule for themselves. It was assumed that language learning meant building up a large repertoire of sentences and grammatical patterns and learning to produce these accurately and quickly in the appropriate situation. Once a basic command of the language was established through oral drilling and controlled practice, the four skills were introduced, usually in the sequence of speaking, listening, read- ing and writing.

Techniques that were often employed included memorization of dialogs, question-and-answer practice, substitution drills, and various forms of guided speaking and writing practice. Great attention to accurate pronunciation and accurate mastery of grammar was stressed from the very beginning stages of language learning, since it was assumed that if students made errors, these would quickly become a permanent part of the learner's speech.

Your turn:
Do you think drills or other forms of repetitive practice should play any role in language teaching?

_____
_____
_____
_____
_____
_____
_____
_____

Methodologies based on these assumptions include **Audiolingualism** (in North America) (also known as the **Aural-Oral Method**), and the **Structural-Situational Approach** in the United Kingdom (also known as **Situational Language Teaching**). Syllabuses during this period consisted of word lists and grammar lists, graded across levels.

In a typical audiolingual lesson, the following procedures would be observed:
1. Students first hear a model dialog (either read by the teacher or on tape) containing key structures that are the focus of the lesson. They repeat each line of the dialog, individually and in chorus. The teacher pays attention to pronunciation, intonation, and fluency. Correction of mistakes of pronunciation or grammar is direct and immediate. The dialog is memorized gradually, line by line. A line may be broken down into several phrases if necessary. The dialog is read aloud in chorus, one half saying one

speaker's part and the other half responding. The students do not consult their book throughout this phase.

2. The dialog is adapted to the students' interest or situation, through changing certain key words or phrases. This is acted out by the students.

3. Certain key structures from the dialog are selected and used as the basis for pattern drills of different kinds. These are first practiced in chorus and then individually. Some grammatical explanation may be offered at this point, but this is kept to an absolute minimum.

4. The students may refer to their textbook, and follow-up reading, writing, or vocabulary activities based on the dialog may be introduced.

5. Follow-up activities may take place in the language laboratory, where further dialog and drill work is carried out.

(Richards and Rodgers 2001, 64–65)

In a typical lesson according to the situational approach, a three-phase sequence, known as the *P-P-P cycle*, was often employed: Presentation, Practice, Production.

Presentation: The new grammar structure is presented, often by means of a conversation or short text. The teacher explains the new structure and checks students' comprehension of it.

Practice: Students practice using the new structure in a controlled context, through drills or substitution exercises.

Production: Students practice using the new structure in different contexts, often using their own content or information, in order to develop fluency with the new pattern.

The P-P-P lesson structure has been widely used in language teaching materials and continues in modified form to be used today. Many speaking- or grammar-based lessons in contemporary materials, for example, begin with an introductory phase in which new teaching points are presented and illustrated in some way and where the focus is on comprehension and recognition. Examples of the new teaching point are given in different contexts. This is often followed by a second phase in which the students practice using the new teaching point in a controlled context using content often provided by the teacher. The third phase is a free practice period during which students try out the teaching point in a free context and in which real or simulated communication is the focus.

The P-P-P lesson format and the assumptions on which it is based have been strongly criticized in recent years, however. Skehan (1996, p.18), for example, comments:

"The underlying theory for a P-P-P approach has now been discredited. The belief that a precise focus on a particular form leads to learning and automatization (that learners will learn what is taught in the order in which it is taught) no longer carries much credibility in linguistics or psychology."

Under the influence of CLT theory, grammar-based methodologies such as the P-P-P have given way to functional and skills-based teaching, and accuracy activities such as drill and grammar practice have been replaced by flu- ency activities based on interactive small-group work. This led to the emergence of a "fluency-first" pedagogy (Brumfit 1984) in which students' grammar needs are determined on the basis of performance on fluency tasks rather than predetermined by a grammatical syllabus. We can distinguish two phases in this development, which we will call *classic communicative language teaching and current communicative language teaching.*

Phase 2: Classic Communicative Language Teaching (1970s to 1990s)

In the 1970s, a reaction to traditional language teaching approaches began and soon spread around the world as older methods such as Audiolingualism and Situational Language Teaching fell out of fashion. The centrality of grammar in language teaching and learning was questioned, since it was argued that language ability involved much more than grammatical competence. While grammatical competence was needed to produce grammatically correct sentences, attention shifted to the knowledge and skills needed to use grammar and other aspects of language appropriately for different communicative purposes such as making requests, giving advice, making suggestions, describing wishes and needs, and so on. What was needed in order to use language communicatively was *communicative competence*. This was a broader concept than that of grammatical competence, and as we saw in Chapter 1, included knowing what to say and how to say it appropriately based on the situation, the participants, and their roles and intentions. Traditional grammatical and vocabulary syllabuses and teaching methods did not include information of this kind. It was assumed that this kind of knowledge would be picked up informally.

The notion of communicative competence was developed within the discipline of linguistics (or more accurately, the subdiscipline of sociolinguistics) and appealed to many within the language teaching profession, who argued that communicative competence, and not simply grammatical competence, should be the goal of language teaching. The next question to be solved was, what would a syllabus that reflected the notion of communicative competence look like and what implications would it have for language teaching methodology? The result was communicative language teaching.

Communicative language teaching created a great deal of enthusiasm and excitement when it first appeared as a new approach to language teaching in the 1970s and 1980s, and language teachers and teaching institutions all around the world soon began to rethink their teaching, syllabuses, and classroom materials. In planning language courses within a communicative approach, grammar was no longer the starting point. New approaches to language teaching were needed. Rather than simply specifying the grammar and vocabulary learners needed to master, it was argued that a syllabus should identify the following aspects of language use in order to be able to develop the learner's communicative competence:

1. As detailed a consideration as possible of the **purposes** for which the learner wishes to acquire the target language; for example, using English for business purposes, in the hotel industry, or for travel.
2. Some idea of the setting in which they will want to use the target language; for example, in an office, on an airplane, or in a store.
3. The socially defined role the learners will assume in the target language, as well as the role of their interlocutors; for example, as a traveler, as a salesperson talking to clients, or as a student in a school.
4. The communicative events in which the learners will participate: everyday situations, vocational or professional situations, academic situations, and so on; for example, making telephone calls, engaging in casual conversation, or taking part in a meeting
5. The language functions involved in those events, or what the learner will be able to do with or through the language; for

example, making introductions, giving explanations, or describing plans

6. The notions or concepts involved, or what the learner will need to be able to talk about; for example, leisure, finance, history, religion.
7. The skills involved in the "knitting together" of discourse: discourse and rhetorical skills; for example, storytelling, giving an effective business presentation.
8. The variety or varieties of the target language that will be needed, such as American, Australian, or British English, and the levels in the spoken and written language which the learners will need to reach.
9. The grammatical content that will be needed.
10. The lexical content, or vocabulary, that will be needed.

(van Ek and Alexander 1980)

This revolution in methodology of language teaching led to two important new directions in the 1970s and 1980s – proposals for a communicative syllabus, and the **ESP** movement.

Proposals for Communicative Syllabus

A traditional language syllabus usually specified the vocabulary students needed to learn and the grammatical items they should master, normally graded across levels from beginner to advanced. But what would a communicative syllabus look like? Several new syllabus types were proposed by advocates of CLT. These included:

Skills-based syllabus

This focuses on the four skills of reading, writing, lis- tening, and speaking, and breaks each skill down into its component microskills. For example, the skill of listening might be further described in terms of the following microskills:

- Recognizing key words in conversations;
- Recognizing the topic of a conversation;
- Recognizing speakers' attitude toward a topic;
- Recognizing time reference of an utterance;

- Following speech at different rates of speed;
- Identifying key information in a passage.

Advocates of CLT, however, stressed an integrated-skills approach to the teaching of the skills. Since in real life the skills often occur together, they should also be linked in teaching, it was argued.

Functional syllabus

This is organized according to the functions the learner should be able to carry out in English, such as expressing likes and dislikes, offering and accepting apologies, introducing someone, and giving explana- tions. Communicative competence is viewed as mastery of functions needed for communication across a wide range of situations. Vocabulary and grammar are then chosen according to the functions being taught. A sequence of activi- ties similar to the P-P-P lesson cycle is then used to present and practice the function. Functional syllabuses were often used as the basis for speaking and listening courses.

Other syllabus types were also proposed at this time. A notional syl- labus was one based around the content and notions a learner would need to express, and a task syllabus specified the tasks and activities students should carry out in the classroom. It was soon realized, however, that a syllabus needs to identify all the relevant components of a language, and the first widely adopted communicative syllabus developed within the framework of classic CLT was termed Threshold Level (Van Ek and Alexander 1980). It described the level of proficiency learners needed to attain to cross the threshold and begin real communication. The threshold syllabus hence specifies topics, functions, notions, situations, as well as grammar and vocabulary.

Your turn:

What are some advantages and disadvantages of a skills-based syllabus and a functional syllabus?

Skills-Based Syllabus

Advantages	***Disadvantages***

Functional Syllabus

Advantages	Disadvantages

English for Specific Purposes

Advocates of CLT also recognized that many learners needed English in order to use it in specific occupational or educational settings. For them it would be more efficient to teach them the specific kinds of language and communicative skills needed for particular roles, (e.g., that of nurse, engineer, flight attendant, pilot, biologist, etc.) rather than just to concentrate on more general English. This led to the discipline of needs analysis – the use of observation, surveys, interviews, situation analysis, and analysis of language samples collected in dif- ferent settings – in order to determine the kinds of communication learners would need to master if they were in specific occupational or educational roles and the language features of particular settings. The focus of needs analysis is to determine the specific characteristics of a language when it is used for specific rather than general purposes. Such differences might include:

- Differences in vocabulary choice
- Differences in grammar
- Differences in the kinds of texts commonly occurring
- Differences in functions
- Differences in the need for particular skills

ESP courses soon began to appear addressing the language needs of university students, nurses, engineers, restaurant staff, doctors, hotel staff, airline pilots, and so on.

Your turn:

Imagine you were developing a course in English for tour guides. In order to carry out a needs analysis as part of the course preparation:

- *Who would you contact?*
- *What kinds of information would you seek to obtain from each contact group?*
- *How would you collect information from them?*

Implications for Methodology

As well as rethinking the nature of a syllabus, the new communicative approach to teaching prompted a rethinking of classroom teaching methodology. It was argued that learners learn a language through the process of communicating in it, and that communication that is meaningful to the learner provides a better opportunity for learning than through a grammar-based approach. The over- arching principles of communicative language teaching methodology at this time can be summarized as follows:

- Make real communication the focus of language learning.
- Provide opportunities for learners to experiment and try out what they know.
- Be tolerant of learners' errors as they indicate that the learner is building up his or her communicative competence.
- Provide opportunities for learners to develop both accuracy and fluency.
- Link the different skills such as speaking, reading, and listening together, since they usually occur so in the real world.
- Let students induce or discover grammar rules.

In applying these principles in the classroom, new classroom techniques and activities were needed, and as we saw above, new roles for teachers and learners in the classroom. Instead of making use of activities that demanded accurate repetition and memorization of sentences and grammatical patterns, activities that required learners to negotiate meaning and to interact meaningfully were required. These activities form the focus of the next chapter.

CHAPTER III. FUNDAMENTALS OF COMMUNICATIVE LANGUAGE TEACHING

Communicative Language Teaching seeks to create a dynamic and learner-centered language education environment where communication is the driving force behind language acquisition. This approach has influenced language teaching practices worldwide, promoting a more communicative and interactive approach to language learning. While there isn't a fixed set of universally agreed-upon fundamental principles for this methodology, we can provide you with several key principles and characteristics that are commonly associated with CLT. These fundamentals capture the essence of the approach and guide language teaching practices centered around communication. Here are 12 key aspects often considered fundamental to CLT:

1. Communication as the Goal.
2. Authentic Language Use.
3. Real-Life Contexts.
4. Task-Based Learning.
5. Student-Centered Approach.
6. Contextual Learning.
7. Language Functions Over Structures.
8. Cultural Sensitivity.
9. Error Tolerance.
10. Interactive Communication.
11. Use of Technology.
12. Assessment through Performance.

It's important to note that the principles of CLT can be adapted and implemented in various ways, and the specifics may vary based on the context, learners' needs, and teaching goals. The essence of CLT lies in its commitment to creating a communicative and interactive language learning environment. Now, we will analyze them in detail.

Fundamental 1. Communication as the Goal

Communicative Language Teaching (CLT) has redefined language education by prioritizing effective communication as the primary goal. The primary objective of CLT, which is to develop communicative competence, serves as a guiding principle, emphasizing the importance of developing learners' ability to use language authentically in real-world situations.

Theoretical Foundations

The theoretical underpinnings of communication as the goal can be linked to **Krashen's Input Hypothesis**. Krashen posited that language acquisition is most effective when learners are exposed to language input that is slightly beyond their current proficiency level, encouraging meaningful communication. Furthermore, **Vygotsky's sociocultural theory** supports the notion that language learning is a social activity. Communication within meaningful social contexts is seen as essential for cognitive development and language acquisition.

Empirical Evidence

Numerous studies have demonstrated **the effectiveness of task-based learning** in enhancing communicative competence. Tasks that require communication in real-life situations have been shown to promote language acquisition and proficiency. Besides, **immersive language learning environments**, where communication is the primary focus, have consistently yielded positive outcomes. Learners engaged in authentic language use within immersive contexts demonstrate improved speaking and listening skills.

Practical Implications

The practical implications of this principle can be as follows:
- Role of the Teacher as Facilitator. Teachers play a facilitative role, guiding students in communicative activities and creating an environment that encourages language use.
- Promotion of Collaborative Learning. Collaborative activities, such as group discussions and pair work, should be incorporated to foster communication and peer interaction.

- Authentic Language Tasks. Design tasks that mirror real-life communication, prompting students to use language authentically to achieve meaningful objectives.
- Feedback and Reflection, in which language teachers should provide constructive feedback on language use, emphasizing effective communication. Reflection sessions allow students to analyze their communication strategies and make improvements.

Model Lesson Plan 1

EXPRESSING OPINIONS

Objective: To develop students' ability to express opinions and engage in discussions.

The Procedure follows the steps below, in which teachers should:

1. Begin with a brief discussion on the importance of expressing opinions in daily life.
2. Introduce a relevant topic or issue that sparks opinions (e.g., environmental conservation).
3. Divide the class into small groups and provide prompts for discussion. Each group discusses the topic, expressing opinions, and presenting arguments.
4. Conclude with a whole-class discussion, encouraging students to use varied expressions to agree, disagree, or express uncertainty.

Model Lesson Plan 2

TRAVEL DIARIES

Objective: To enhance students' descriptive language skills through the creation of travel diaries.

The Procedure follows the steps below, in which teachers should:

1. Discuss the concept of travel diaries and their purpose in sharing experiences.
2. Have students recall a recent trip or plan an imaginary one. In pairs, students create a travel diary entry, describing their experiences, feelings, and impressions.
3. Encourage the use of vivid and descriptive language to convey the travel narrative. Students share their travel diaries with the class, fostering communication and language expression.

Model Lesson Plan 3

EVERYDAY COMMUNICATION SKILLS

Objective: To enhance students' ability to engage in everyday conversations using appropriate language expressions.

The Procedure follows the steps below, in which teachers should:

1. Begin with a discussion on the importance of effective communication in daily life.
2. Introduce common scenarios (e.g., ordering food, making small talk) where authentic conversations occur.
3. Provide students with role cards depicting different characters in these scenarios. Students pair up and engage in role-playing conversations based on the given scenarios.
4. Facilitate a class discussion on the challenges faced, successful communication strategies, and language used during
5. the role-play.

CHAPTER III. FUNDAMENTALS OF COMMUNICATIVE LANGUAGE TEACHING

Model Lesson Plan 4

COLLABORATIVE STORYTELLING

Objective: To develop students' narrative skills through collaborative storytelling.

The Procedure follows the steps below, in which teachers should:
1. Discuss the power of storytelling and its role in effective communication.
2. Form small groups and assign each group a starting point for a story. Each student in the group contributes a sentence or paragraph to the evolving story.
3. Encourage the use of cohesive devices and effective communication to maintain coherence. Groups share their collaborative stories with the class, fostering communication and narrative proficiency.

As we can see, the principle "Communication as the Goal" in CLT represents a paradigm shift in language education, emphasizing the development of communicative competence. The theoretical foundations, empirical evidence, and model lesson plans presented in this scientific exploration highlight the centrality of effective communication in language learning. As educators continue to shape language classrooms, the commitment to communication as the ultimate goal serves as a compass, guiding the creation of engaging, meaningful, and communicative language learning experiences. This scientific inquiry contributes to a nuanced understanding of the multifaceted dimensions of communication within the CLT framework.

Fundamental 2. Authentic Language Use

Authentic language use stands as a cornerstone in Communicative Language Teaching (CLT), emphasizing the importance of exposing learners to real-world language contexts as the xposure to authentic language materials, such as real-world texts, videos, and audio recordings, provides learners with a genuine understanding of language use.

Theoretical Foundations

Vygotsky's sociocultural theory posits that learning is a social activity, and language development is deeply intertwined with cultural experiences. Authentic language use, reflecting genuine cultural and social contexts, aligns seamlessly with this theoretical framework. Furthermore, the **functional notional approach** emphasizes teaching language in functional, communicative units rather than isolated grammar rules. Authentic language use integrates these functional elements, providing learners with tools for real-world communication.

Empirical Evidence

Studies have consistently shown that exposure to authentic materials, such as videos, podcasts, and real-life texts, contributes significantly to **vocabulary acquisition**. Learners engaged in authentic language contexts demonstrate a richer and more nuanced vocabulary.Besides, **immersive language learning environments**, where authentic language use is prioritized, have been shown to accelerate language proficiency. Learners immersed in real-world language contexts exhibit improved listening comprehension, speaking fluency, and overall communicative competence.

Practical Implications

The practical implications of this principle can be as follows:

- **Integration of Multimedia Resources.** Authentic language use is enriched by multimedia resources. Educators should integrate videos, podcasts, and online articles to expose learners to diverse accents, linguistic variations, and authentic language registers.
- **Cultural Sensitivity and Awareness.** Model lesson plans should embed cultural elements, fostering learners' cultural sensitivity and

awareness. This includes exposure to different cultural norms, customs, and communication styles.

- **Task-Based Learning.** Design tasks that simulate real-life situations, prompting students to use language authentically to achieve specific goals. This can include role-plays, problem-solving tasks, or collaborative projects.

- **Authentic Assessment Measures.** Assessments should reflect real-life language use. Include tasks such as presenting information, engaging in debates, or writing authentic texts to evaluate learners' communicative competence.

Model Lesson Plan 1

REAL-LIFE CONVERSATIONS

Objective: To enhance students' conversational skills in authentic social situations.

The Procedure follows the steps below, in which teachers should:

1. Introduce a topic relevant to everyday life, such as making introductions or discussing hobbies.
2. Provide students with real-life scenarios, like social gatherings or networking events. In pairs or small groups, students engage in authentic conversations based on the given scenarios.
3. Encourage the use of conversational strategies and appropriate language expressions.
4. Conclude with a debriefing session, allowing students to reflect
on the challenges and successes in authentic communication.

Model Lesson Plan 2

> **CULTURAL EXPLORATION THROUGH AUTHENTIC TEXTS**
>
> **Objective:** To develop cultural awareness and language proficiency through authentic texts.
>
> **The Procedure** follows the steps below, in which teachers should:
>
> 1. Select authentic texts from diverse cultural sources, such as newspapers, blogs, or literature.
> 2. Assign texts that provide insights into cultural practices, traditions, or contemporary issues. In class, students read and analyze the texts, focusing on language use and cultural nuances.
> 3. Facilitate group discussions where students share their interpretations and reflections.
> 4. Conclude with a collaborative project where students create presentations or reports, integrating their findings into authentic language use.

It is obvious that the principle "Authentic Language Use" in CLT represents a transformative approach to language education, fostering not only linguistic proficiency but also cultural understanding. The theoretical foundations, empirical insights, and model lesson plans presented in this scientific exploration underscore the significance of integrating authentic language use into language classrooms. As educators navigate the evolving landscape of language instruction, the commitment to authentic language use serves as a catalyst for creating engaging, relevant, and culturally rich language learning experiences. This scientific inquiry contributes to a deeper understanding of the multifaceted dimensions of authentic language use within the CLT framework.

CHAPTER III. FUNDAMENTALS OF COMMUNICATIVE LANGUAGE TEACHING

Fundamental 3. Real-Life Contexts

Communicative Language Teaching (CLT) revolutionizes language education by emphasizing the importance of "Real-Life Contexts." At the heart of this approach is the belief that language is most effectively acquired when learners engage with it in authentic situations, which allows learners to understand and use the language in situations they might encounter outside the classroom.

Theoretical Foundations:

The theoretical underpinnings of real-life contexts in CLT can be traced to **Vygotsky's sociocultural theory**. This perspective asserts that learning is a social and cultural process, emphasizing the importance of language use in authentic social contexts. Furthermore, Real-life contexts align closely with the principles of **Task-Based Language Teaching**. TBLT posits that language learning is most effective when embedded in purposeful tasks that simulate real-world situations, fostering both language development and problem-solving skills.

Empirical Evidence:

Studies have consistently shown that **exposure to authentic language** in real-life contexts leads to **higher proficiency levels**. Learners engaged in tasks and interactions mirroring daily life demonstrate improved language skills compared to those in more artificial learning environments. Beides, real-life contexts contribute to **cultural sensitivity and integration**. Research indicates that learners exposed to language within authentic cultural settings are better equipped to understand and navigate cultural nuances in communication.

Practical Implications

The practical implications of this principle can be as follows:
- **Task-Based Learning (TBL).** Implement task-based learning activities that mirror real-life scenarios, enabling students to use language in purposeful tasks and interactions.
- **Role-Playing.** Incorporate role-playing activities where students take on different roles in familiar situations, promoting authentic language use and interpersonal communication skills.

- **Realia and Authentic Materials.** Integrate realia, authentic texts, and multimedia materials that reflect real-life contexts into lessons to expose students to genuine language use.
- **Cultural Exploration.** Infuse cultural elements into lessons to broaden students' cultural awareness and sensitivity, allowing them to navigate diverse language contexts.

Model Lesson Plan 1:

EVERYDAY CONVERSATIONS

Objective: To develop students' ability to engage in everyday conversations using appropriate language expressions.

The Procedure follows the steps below, in which teachers should:

1. Begin with a discussion on the importance of effective communication in daily life.
2. Introduce a set of common scenarios (e.g., ordering food, making small talk, asking for directions) where authentic conversations occur.
3. Provide students with role cards depicting different characters in these scenarios. Students pair up and engage in role-playing conversations based on the given scenarios.
4. Facilitate a class discussion on the challenges faced, successful communication strategies, and language used during the role-play.

Model Lesson Plan 2

> ### TRAVEL PLANNING
>
> **Objective:** To enhance students' language skills in the context of planning a trip.
>
> **The Procedure** follows the steps below, in which teachers should:
>
> 1. Discuss the relevance of trip planning and the language involved (e.g., making reservations, discussing itineraries).
> 2. Divide the class into small groups and assign each group a travel destination. Students research and plan a trip to their assigned destination, considering accommodation, transportation, and activities. Groups present their travel plans to the class using the target language, emphasizing effective communication.
> 3. Conclude with a reflection on the language skills developed during the task and potential challenges in real travel situations.

In conclusion, "Real-Life Contexts" in CLT represents a transformative approach to language education, emphasizing the acquisition of language skills within authentic, everyday situations. The theoretical foundations, empirical evidence, and practical examples presented in this scientific exploration underscore the significance of integrating real-life contexts into language classrooms. As educators strive to create dynamic and engaging learning environments, the commitment to real-life contexts serves as a guiding principle in fostering communicative competence and cultural understanding. This scientific inquiry contributes to a deeper understanding of the multifaceted dimensions of real-life contexts within the CLT framework.

Fundamental 4. Task-Based Learning

Task-Based Learning (TBL) has emerged as a central tenet of Communicative Language Teaching (CLT), emphasizing the use of language in purposeful tasks to promote meaningful communication. By understanding and incorporating task-based learning, educators can foster a dynamic and student-centered language learning environment because learning activities are organized around tasks that require meaningful communication and problem-solving, promoting language use in purposeful contexts.

Theoretical Foundations

Task-based learning aligns with **Vygotsky's sociocultural theory**, emphasizing the social nature of language development. TBL provides opportunities for collaborative learning, allowing students to engage in authentic language use within a social context. Furthermore, theoretical frameworks within CLT, such as **Hymes' concept of communicative competence**, advocate for language learning that goes beyond grammatical rules. TBL focuses on developing learners' ability to use language in real-life situations, contributing to communicative competence.

Empirical Evidence:

Research studies consistently demonstrate the **positive impact of task-based learning** on language proficiency. TBL fosters the development of listening, speaking, reading, and writing skills, resulting in well-rounded language competence. Besides, empirical evidence indicates that TBL enhances **learner motivation and engagement**. The incorporation of purposeful tasks creates a dynamic learning environment, encouraging active participation and sustained interest.

Practical Implications

The practical implications of this principle can be as follows:

Variety of Task Types. Incorporate a variety of task types, including information gap tasks, problem-solving tasks, and opinion-sharing tasks, to cater to different language learning objectives.

Authentic Materials and Realia, in which language teachers can use authentic materials and realia to enhance task authenticity. For example, provide authentic maps, brochures, or menus for travel planning or restaurant scenarios.

Feedback and Reflection, in which language teachers can integrate regular feedback sessions and opportunities for student reflection. These processes contribute to a continuous improvement cycle, allowing learners to refine their language use based on constructive feedback.

Assessment Through Performance, in which language teachers can assess students' performance in task-based activities to evaluate their communicative competence. This may include rubrics that assess language accuracy, fluency, and appropriateness in real-life tasks.

Model Lesson Plan 1

RESTAURANT SCENARIO

Objective: To enhance students' ability to communicate effectively in a restaurant setting.

The Procedure follows the steps below, in which teachers should:

1. Begin with a discussion on common scenarios in restaurants and the language required for ordering food, making inquiries, and expressing preferences.
2. Divide the class into small groups and assign each group a role, such as customers, waitstaff, and chefs.
3. Students collaboratively plan and act out a restaurant scenario, incorporating authentic language use.
4. After the role-play, facilitate a debriefing session where students reflect on their communication strategies and language choices.
5. Conclude with a class discussion on the challenges and successes encountered during the task.

Model Lesson Plan 2

TRAVEL ITINERARY PROJECT

Objective: To develop students' language skills in planning and presenting a travel itinerary.

The Procedure follows the steps below, in which teachers should:

1. Introduce the concept of planning a trip and the language associated with making reservations, discussing itineraries, and providing recommendations.
2. In pairs or small groups, assign each group a destination and task them with planning a travel itinerary.
3. Students create a multimedia presentation showcasing their travel plans, incorporating language learned during the lesson.
4. Groups present their travel itineraries to the class, emphasizing effective communication and language proficiency.
5. Conclude with a class discussion on the diverse language skills employed in the presentations.

As we can see, Task-Based Learning stands as a dynamic and effective approach within Communicative Language Teaching, promoting language acquisition through purposeful and authentic tasks. The theoretical foundations, empirical evidence, and model lesson plans presented in this scientific exploration underscore the transformative potential of TBL in language education. As educators navigate the evolving landscape of language instruction, the integration of task-based learning offers a student-centered, engaging, and communicatively rich approach to language learning. This scientific inquiry contributes to a nuanced understanding of the multifaceted dimensions of task-based learning within the CLT framework.

Fundamental 5. Student-Centered Approach

The Student-Centered Approach is a cornerstone of Communicative Language Teaching, placing learners at the heart of the language education process. Within this principle, the teacher serves as a facilitator, and the learning environment is student-centered, encouraging active participation, collaboration, and learner autonomy. By embracing a student-centered approach, educators can create dynamic, personalized, and engaging language learning experiences that cater to the diverse needs of learners.

Theoretical Foundations:

The student-centered approach aligns with **constructivist learning theories**, emphasizing that learners actively construct knowledge through meaningful interactions. Students are encouraged to explore, question, and make connections, fostering a deeper understanding of language concepts.

Furthermore, **autonomous learning** is a key component of the student-centered approach. Drawing from theories of autonomy in language learning, this approach empowers learners to take responsibility for their learning journey, promoting self-directed exploration and decision-making.

Empirical Evidence:

Numerous studies indicate that a student-centered **approach enhances learner motivation and engagement**. When students have a say in their learning processes and are involved in decision-making, they become more invested in the learning experience. Besides, empirical evidence suggests that student-centered classrooms contribute to **improved language proficiency**. Learners engaged in meaningful, personalized activities tend to demonstrate better retention, application, and transfer of language skills.

Practical Implications

The practical implications of this principle can be as follows:
- **Flexible Learning Paths**, in which language teachers should design curricula that allow for flexible learning paths, enabling students to pursue topics of interest and engage with materials that resonate with their preferences.

- **Incorporation of Student Feedback**, in which language teachers should regularly seek feedback from students about their learning experiences. Adjust teaching methods, materials, and activities based on this feedback to better align with students' needs and preferences.

- **Encouragement of Collaborative Learning**, in which language teachers should foster a collaborative learning environment where students can engage in peer-to-peer interactions, collaborative projects, and language activities that promote teamwork and communication.

- **Individualized Assessments**, in which language teachers should implement assessments that take into account the individual progress and achievements of students. This can include portfolio assessments, reflective journals, and personalized projects.

Model Lesson Plan 1

PERSONALIZED LEARNING JOURNALS

Objective: To encourage students to reflect on their language learning progress and set individual goals.

The Procedure follows the steps below, in which teachers should:

1. Introduce the concept of personalized learning journals and their importance in tracking language development.
2. Provide students with journals or digital platforms where they can document their language learning experiences, challenges, and successes.
3. Set aside dedicated time for students to reflect on their progress, set language goals, and plan strategies for improvement.
4. Facilitate periodic one-on-one conferences to discuss students' reflections and provide personalized feedback.
5. Conclude the semester with a reflective session where students share their language learning journeys with the class.

Model Lesson Plan 2

> ### PROJECT-BASED LANGUAGE LEARNING
>
> **Objective:** To engage students in collaborative, project-based language activities that align with their interests.
>
> **The Procedure** follows the steps below, in which teachers should:
>
> 1. Begin by discussing the benefits of project-based learning and how it aligns with a student-centered approach.
> 2. Allow students to choose a project topic related to their interests, such as creating a podcast, writing a blog, or producing a short film.
> 3. Facilitate project planning sessions where students outline goals, timelines, and language skills they aim to develop.
> 4. Provide support and guidance throughout the project, emphasizing language use and communication in the chosen medium.
> 5. Conclude with project presentations, fostering a collaborative and communicative environment.

The Student-Centered Approach within Communicative Language Teaching marks a significant shift toward personalized and engaging language education. The theoretical foundations, empirical evidence, and model lesson plans presented in this scientific exploration underscore the transformative potential of placing students at the center of the learning process. As educators continue to refine their teaching practices, embracing a student-centered approach offers a pathway to creating meaningful, dynamic, and student-focused language learning experiences. This scientific inquiry contributes to a nuanced understanding of the multifaceted dimensions of the student-centered approach within the CLT framework.

Fundamental 6. Contextual Learning

Contextual learning is also a cornerstone of Communicative Language Teaching (CLT), emphasizing the importance of situating language acquisition within authentic, real-world contexts. Within this principle, language is learned in context, with a focus on understanding how language functions in different social and cultural settings. By integrating language learning with contextual understanding, educators can create dynamic and relevant language learning experiences that resonate with learners.

Theoretical Foundations:

Contextual learning aligns with **constructivist learning theories**, which posit that learners actively construct knowledge through meaningful interactions with their environment. Placing language within authentic contexts provides learners with a richer and more holistic understanding of linguistic structures. Furthermore, the concept of **situated learning**, as proposed by Lave and Wenger, suggests that learning is most effective when situated within authentic contexts. Contextual learning in language education reflects this idea, emphasizing the role of authentic situations in language acquisition.

Empirical Evidence:

Studies indicate that learners exposed to contextual learning environments demonstrate **enhanced vocabulary retention**. Embedding language within relevant contexts aids memory retrieval and application of words in real-world situations. Besides, empirical evidence supports the **positive impact** of contextual learning on **communicative competence**. Learners engaged in language activities situated within specific contexts demonstrate higher proficiency in using language for various communicative purposes.

Practical Implications

The practical implications of this principle can be as follows:
- **Realia and Authentic Materials**, in which language teachers should utilize realia, authentic materials, and props to create immersive and authentic learning environments. This can include newspapers, maps,

videos, and other materials that represent genuine language use in specific contexts.

- **Field Trips and Experiential Learning**, in which language teachers should plan field trips or experiential learning activities that expose students to language use in authentic settings. This could involve visits to local businesses, community centers, or cultural events.

- **Technology Integration**, in which language teachers should leverage technology to bring real-world contexts into the classroom. Virtual tours, online resources, and multimedia materials can provide students with exposure to authentic language use in various contexts.

- **Cultural Integration**, in which language teachers should infuse cultural elements into contextual learning activities to broaden students' cultural awareness and sensitivity. This includes exploring language use within diverse cultural settings.

Model Lesson Plan 1

IN THE MARKET

Objective: To enhance students' ability to use language effectively in a market setting.

The Procedure follows the steps below, in which teachers should:

1. Begin with a discussion on common language used in markets, such as bargaining, inquiring about products, and expressing preferences.
2. Create a simulated market environment within the classroom using props, signs, and role-playing scenarios.
3. Divide the class into buyers and sellers. Buyers engage in negotiating prices and making purchases while sellers practice describing products and negotiating.
4. Facilitate a debriefing session, allowing students to reflect on their language use and strategies during the market simulation.
5. Conclude with a collaborative discussion on the challenges and successes encountered in the contextual learning activity.

Model Lesson Plan 2

NEIGHBORHOOD EXPLORATION

Objective: To develop students' language skills for describing and discussing neighborhoods.

The Procedure follows the steps below, in which teachers should:

1. Introduce the theme of neighborhoods and the language used for describing locations, giving directions, and discussing community features.
2. Organize a neighborhood exploration activity where students walk around the local community, observing and noting details.
3. In pairs or small groups, students create presentations describing different aspects of the neighborhood, incorporating language learned in the lesson.
4. Presentations are followed by a question-and-answer session, encouraging students to use descriptive language effectively.
5. Conclude with a reflective discussion on how contextual learning enhanced their understanding of neighborhood-related language.

In conclusion, Contextual learning within Communicative Language Teaching represents a pedagogical approach that elevates language education by grounding it in authentic, real-world contexts. The theoretical foundations, empirical evidence, and model lesson plans presented in this scientific exploration underscore the transformative potential of integrating language learning with contextual understanding. As educators continue to refine their instructional strategies, the commitment to contextual learning offers a pathway to creating dynamic, relevant, and culturally rich language learning experiences. This scientific inquiry contributes to a nuanced understanding of the multifaceted dimensions of contextual learning within the CLT framework.

Fundamental 7. Language Functions over Structures

The paradigm shift in CLT towards prioritizing language functions over structures signifies a departure from traditional grammar-focused language instruction. Within this principle, the emphasis is on language functions (e.g., making requests, giving opinions) rather than isolated grammatical structures, fostering practical language use. By emphasizing language functions, CLT seeks to cultivate learners' ability to communicate meaningfully in real-world situations.

Theoretical Foundations

The functional-notional approach underpins the emphasis on language functions. This approach categorizes language into functions (e.g., requesting, expressing opinions) and notions (e.g., time, quantity) rather than focusing solely on grammatical structures. It aligns with the communicative goals of CLT. Furthermore, **Halliday's Systemic Functional Linguistics theory** posits that language is a social semiotic system, and linguistic choices are made to fulfill specific social functions. Focusing on language functions aligns with the systemic functional linguistics perspective, emphasizing the functional purpose of language in communication.

Empirical Evidence Insights

Studies demonstrate that learners exposed to a language functions approach exhibit **enhanced communication skills**. By emphasizing functional language use, learners become adept at using language in diverse communicative contexts. Besides, learners engaged in activities centered around language functions show **increased motivation and engagement**. Real-world language functions resonate with learners as they perceive the immediate applicability of what they are learning.

Practical Implications

Task-Based Language Teaching (TBLT), in which language teachers should incorporate task-based activities that emphasize language functions in real-world contexts. This could include problem-solving tasks, role-plays, or collaborative projects that require specific language functions.

Integration of Authentic Materials, in which language teachers should use authentic materials such as dialogues, articles, or videos that exemplify language functions in natural communication. This exposes learners to real-world language use and diverse communicative situations.

Student-Centered Learning, in which language teachers should adopt a student-centered approach where learners actively engage in activities that require the application of language functions. This can include discussions, debates, or project-based learning.

Formative Assessment of Language Functions, in which language teachers should design formative assessments that evaluate students' proficiency in using language functions. This could involve role-plays, oral presentations, or written tasks that assess their ability to apply language functions in context.

Model Lesson Plan 1

MAKING SUGGESTIONS

Objective: To develop students' ability to make and respond to suggestions.

The Procedure follows the steps below, in which teachers should:

1. Start with a brief discussion on the importance of making suggestions in various contexts, such as social settings or group projects.
2. Introduce common language functions related to making suggestions (e.g., "How about," "Why don't we").
3. Engage students in pair or group activities where they practice making suggestions and responding appropriately.
4. Facilitate a class discussion on effective suggestion strategies and language use.
5. Conclude with a collaborative task, such as planning an event, where students apply the language functions learned.

CHAPTER III. FUNDAMENTALS OF COMMUNICATIVE LANGUAGE TEACHING

Model Lesson Plan 2

PROBLEM-SOLVING IN THE WORKPLACE

Objective: To enhance students' problem-solving skills using appropriate language functions.

The Procedure follows the steps below, in which teachers should:

1. Discuss the importance of effective communication in problem-solving within a workplace context.
2. Introduce language functions related to proposing solutions, expressing agreement or disagreement, and negotiating.
3. Provide case studies or scenarios related to workplace challenges.
4. In pairs or small groups, students engage in role-playing activities where they apply language functions to address the presented challenges.
5. Conclude with a reflection session, allowing students to analyze the effectiveness of language functions in problem-solving situations.

Prioritizing language functions over structures in CLT represents a pedagogical shift that aligns language education with authentic communication. The theoretical foundations, empirical insights, and model lesson plans presented in this scientific exploration underscore the transformative potential of focusing on language functions. As educators continue to refine their instructional approaches, embracing a language functions approach offers a pathway to creating meaningful, communicative, and proficiency-driven language learning experiences. This scientific inquiry contributes to a nuanced understanding of the multifaceted dimensions of language functions within the CLT framework.

Fundamental 8. Cultural Sensitivity

Cultural sensitivity is a crucial dimension of Communicative Language Teaching (CLT), emphasizing the importance of integrating cultural awareness into language education. Within this principle, cultural elements are integrated into lessons to help learners understand and navigate cultural nuances in language use. By fostering cultural sensitivity, CLT aims to prepare learners for meaningful engagement in a diverse and interconnected world.

Theoretical Foundations

The concept of **Intercultural Communicative Competence (ICC)**, as proposed by Byram, underlies the importance of cultural sensitivity. It emphasizes the ability to interact effectively and appropriately with speakers of other languages and cultures, transcending linguistic competence alone. Furthermore, **Vygotsky's sociocultural theory** suggests that language development is intertwined with cultural and social experiences. Cultural sensitivity in language education aligns with this theory by acknowledging the role of culture in shaping language use and communication.

Empirical Insights

Research indicates that learners who are culturally sensitive demonstrate **enhanced communication skills** in diverse contexts. Cultural sensitivity fosters an understanding of cultural nuances, leading to more effective and context-appropriate communication. Besides, empirical evidence suggests that exposure to culturally sensitive language education **promotes open-mindedness and empathy**. Learners develop a greater appreciation for diverse perspectives, contributing to a more inclusive and understanding global community.

Practical Implications

Incorporation of Diverse Cultural Materials, in which language teachers should integrate diverse cultural materials, such as literature, music, films, and authentic texts, into language instruction. Exposure to a variety of cultural expressions broadens learners' perspectives and enhances cultural sensitivity.

Language Exchange Programs, in which language teachers should organize language exchange programs or collaborative projects with learners from different cultural backgrounds. This provides opportunities for authentic cross-cultural communication and fosters cultural sensitivity.

Cross-Cultural Dialogues, in which language teachers should facilitate cross-cultural dialogues within the classroom. Structured discussions on cultural topics, values, and norms allow learners to engage in meaningful conversations that promote cultural sensitivity.

Cultural Competence Assessment, in which language teachers should develop assessments that gauge learners' cultural competence. This could include projects, presentations, or reflective assignments that assess their ability to navigate cultural nuances in language use.

Model Lesson Plan 1

CULTURAL EXCHANGE PROJECT

Objective: To promote cultural sensitivity through collaborative research and presentations.

The Procedure follows the steps below, in which teachers should:

1. Divide the class into small groups, each focusing on a specific country or cultural group.
2. Instruct students to research and gather information about the chosen culture, including language, customs, traditions, and societal norms.
3. Each group prepares a presentation showcasing their findings, emphasizing the importance of cultural sensitivity in communication.
4. Presentations are followed by a Q&A session where students engage in cross-cultural dialogue.
5. Conclude with a reflective discussion on the impact of cultural sensitivity in effective communication.

Model Lesson Plan 2

> ### MULTILINGUAL STORYTELLING
>
> **Objective:** To encourage cultural sensitivity through the exploration of multilingual storytelling.
>
> **The Procedure** follows the steps below, in which teachers should:
>
> 1. Introduce the concept of multilingual storytelling and its role in preserving cultural narratives.
> 2. Invite students to share stories from their cultural backgrounds, emphasizing the use of their native languages alongside the target language.
> 3. Facilitate a collaborative storytelling session where students contribute to a multilingual story, incorporating cultural elements.
> 4. Encourage discussions on the cultural significance of language use and storytelling.
> 5. Conclude with a reflection on how multilingual storytelling promotes cultural sensitivity and appreciation.

Cultural sensitivity in Communicative Language Teaching is not merely an additional component but a fundamental principle that enhances the effectiveness of language education. The theoretical foundations, empirical insights, and model lesson plans presented in this scientific exploration underscore the transformative potential of integrating cultural sensitivity into language instruction. As educators continue to shape the language learning landscape, the commitment to fostering cultural sensitivity contributes to the development of global citizens capable of navigating diverse linguistic and cultural contexts. This scientific inquiry adds depth to our understanding of the multifaceted dimensions of cultural sensitivity within the CLT framework.

CHAPTER III. FUNDAMENTALS OF COMMUNICATIVE LANGUAGE TEACHING

Fundamental 9. Error Tolerance

Error tolerance is a pivotal aspect of Communicative Language Teaching, acknowledging that errors are an inherent part of the language learning process. Within this principle, learners are encouraged to take risks and communicate, even if it means making mistakes. Errors are viewed as opportunities for learning and improvement. By embracing error tolerance, CLT aims to cultivate a supportive learning environment where learners are encouraged to take risks, communicate freely, and learn from their linguistic mistakes.

Theoretical Foundations:

The concept of **Vygotsky's Zone of Proximal Development (ZPD)** suggests that learners can advance their language skills with support just beyond their current proficiency level. Error tolerance aligns with this theory by allowing learners to experiment with language without fear of harsh judgment, fostering an environment conducive to language development. Furthermore, **Krashen's Input Hypothesis** posits that language acquisition occurs when learners are exposed to comprehensible input slightly beyond their current proficiency. Error tolerance supports this hypothesis by allowing learners to produce language, even if it contains errors, as part of the natural learning process.

Empirical Insights:

Research indicates that a tolerant attitude toward errors in language learning **reduces anxiety levels** among learners. When students feel less pressured to be error-free, they are **more motivated** to participate actively in language activities and take risks in communication. Besides, Empirical evidence suggests that learners who experience error tolerance demonstrate **improved language accuracy over time**. The freedom to make mistakes and receive constructive feedback contributes to a more nuanced understanding of language rules and structures.

Practical Implications

The practical applications of this principle can be as follows:
- **Constructive Feedback Strategies**, in which educators should adopt constructive feedback strategies that emphasize the importance of

errors as opportunities for learning. Feedback should focus on guiding learners toward the correct usage rather than punitive correction.

- **Peer Collaboration**, in which we should encourage peer collaboration and the sharing of experiences related to language learning. Peer support creates a community where learners feel comfortable taking risks and learning from each other's mistakes.
- **Error Journals**, in which language teachers should implement error journals where students can document and reflect on the errors they make during language tasks. This practice encourages self-awareness and active engagement with language improvement.
- **Incorporation of Error Analysis Tasks**, in which language teachers should design language tasks specifically aimed at error analysis. These tasks allow students to explore common errors, understand patterns, and work collaboratively to correct and improve language usage.

Model Lesson Plan 1

ERROR ANALYSIS AND CORRECTION

Objective: To encourage self-reflection and correction of language errors.

The Procedure follows the steps below, in which teachers should:

1. Begin with a discussion on the importance of learning from mistakes and fostering a supportive learning environment.
2. Assign a language task or writing assignment where students are likely to make errors.
3. After completing the task, instruct students to analyze their own work, identifying errors and reflecting on potential corrections.
4. In pairs or small groups, students discuss their findings and collaboratively work on correcting errors.
5. Conclude with a class reflection on the value of self-correction and the role of error tolerance in the learning process.

Model Lesson Plan 2

> **ERROR TOLERANCE IN ORAL PRESENTATIONS**
>
> **Objective:** To create a supportive environment for learners to engage in oral presentations without fear of errors.
>
> **The Procedure** follows the steps below, in which teachers should:
>
> 1. Discuss the significance of oral communication skills in language learning and the role of error tolerance in fostering a positive learning atmosphere.
> 2. Assign topics for short oral presentations, encouraging students to express their ideas freely.
> 3. Emphasize that the focus is on effective communication rather than perfect language use.
> 4. After presentations, facilitate a feedback session where peers provide constructive feedback on content and delivery without overly focusing on linguistic errors.
> 5. Conclude with a class discussion on the benefits of an error-tolerant environment for oral communication.

Error tolerance in Communicative Language Teaching represents a fundamental shift towards creating a positive and supportive learning environment. The theoretical foundations, empirical insights, and model lesson plans presented in this scientific exploration underscore the transformative potential of embracing errors as an integral part of the language learning journey. As educators continue to refine their instructional approaches, a commitment to error tolerance contributes to the development of resilient, motivated, and proficient language learners. This scientific inquiry adds depth to our understanding of the multifaceted dimensions of error tolerance within the CLT framework.

Fundamental 10. Interactive Communication

Interactive communication is at the core of Communicative Language Teaching, emphasizing the importance of language use in authentic and meaningful interactions. Within this principle, Activities promote interactive communication, encouraging learners to engage in conversations, discussions, and collaborative tasks. By prioritizing interactive communication, CLT aims to prepare learners for effective language use in diverse and dynamic social contexts.

Theoretical Frameworks:

The concept of **communicative competence**, as proposed by Hymes, underlies the importance of interactive communication. It extends beyond linguistic competence to include the ability to use language appropriately in various social situations. Furthermore, **the Transactional Model of Communication** views communication as an exchange where participants actively engage in sending and receiving messages. Interactive communication aligns with this model, emphasizing the dynamic nature of language use.

Practical Applications:

The practical applications of this principle can be as follows:

- **Pair and Group Activities**, in which language teachers should incorporate pair and group activities that require students to engage in interactive communication. These activities can include role-plays, discussions, and collaborative projects that promote active language use.
- **Real-life Scenarios**, in which language teachers should introduce real-life scenarios that prompt interactive communication. Simulated situations such as ordering food in a restaurant, asking for directions, or participating in job interviews provide opportunities for practical language application.

Practical Implications:

- **Variety in Interaction Patterns**, in which language teachers should incorporate a variety of interaction patterns, including pair work, group discussions, and whole-class interactions. Diversifying interaction patterns caters to different learning preferences and promotes overall language development.

- **Authentic Materials**, in which language teachers should utilize authentic materials such as videos, podcasts, or interviews that showcase real-life interactive communication. This exposes learners to natural language use and diverse communicative styles.
- **Task-Based Learning**, in which language teachers should implement task-based learning activities that necessitate interactive communication to achieve a goal. Task-oriented projects encourage collaboration and meaningful language use.
- **Technology Integration**, in which language teachers should leverage technology to facilitate interactive communication. Virtual platforms, discussion forums, and video conferencing tools can enhance language practice beyond the traditional classroom setting.

Model Lesson Plan 1

TRAVEL DIALOGUE SIMULATION

Objective: To develop interactive communication skills in a travel-related context.

The Procedure follows the steps below, in which teachers should:

1. Begin with a discussion on common travel scenarios and the language needed for effective communication.
2. Divide the class into pairs, assigning each pair a travel scenario (e.g., asking for directions, booking accommodation).
3. In each pair, one student takes on the role of a traveler, and the other assumes the role of a local guide or service provider.
4. Students engage in role-playing the travel scenario, using language learned in the lesson.
5. Rotate roles and scenarios to provide diverse interactive experiences.
6. Conclude with a debriefing session where students reflect on the challenges and successes of the interactive communication task.

Model Lesson Plan 2

> ### GROUP PROBLEM-SOLVING ACTIVITY
>
> **Objective:** To enhance interactive communication through collaborative problem-solving.
>
> **The Procedure** follows the steps below, in which teachers should:
> 1. Present a real-life problem or scenario relevant to the learners' interests or experiences.
> 2. Divide the class into small groups and assign each group the task of collaboratively solving the presented problem.
> 3. Encourage groups to use language creatively and interactively to discuss and propose solutions.
> 4. Facilitate a group discussion where each team presents its solution and engages in dialogue with other groups.
> 5. Conclude with a reflection session, emphasizing the importance of interactive communication in problem-solving.

Interactive communication stands as one of the cornerstones of Communicative Language Teaching, fostering language proficiency through dynamic and authentic language use. The theoretical frameworks, practical applications, and model lesson plans presented in this scientific exploration underscore the transformative potential of prioritizing interactive communication in language education. As educators continue to refine their teaching practices, the commitment to fostering interactive communication offers a pathway to creating communicatively competent and socially adept language learners. This scientific inquiry contributes to a nuanced understanding of the multifaceted dimensions of interactive communication within the CLT framework.

Fundamental 11. Use of Technology

The integration of technology in language education is a key dimension of Communicative Language Teaching (CLT), reflecting the need to align language instruction with the realities of the digital age. Within this principle, technology is integrated into language teaching to enhance learning experiences, provide authentic materials, and facilitate communication. By incorporating technology, CLT aims to engage learners in dynamic and interactive language experiences, fostering communicative competence in the digital era.

Theoretical Foundations

Technology integration aligns with **socio-cultural learning theories**, emphasizing the importance of social interactions and collaborative learning. Digital tools facilitate communication and collaboration beyond the confines of the traditional classroom. Furthermore, the **multimodal learning theory** recognizes that learners benefit from exposure to diverse modes of representation. Technology provides opportunities for incorporating visual, auditory, and interactive elements, catering to different learning styles.

Practical Strategies

Interactive Language Apps, in which language teachers can utilize language learning applications that provide interactive exercises, gamified activities, and multimedia content. Apps like **Duolingo**, **Babbel**, **Rosetta Stone** or **Ibrat Academy** offer learners a dynamic and personalized language learning experience.

Virtual Reality (VR) Language Immersion, by which language teachers can implement virtual reality experiences to immerse learners in authentic language environments. Virtual field trips, language immersion apps, or VR language exchange platforms enable learners to explore language in context.

Practical Implications

Blended Learning Environments, in which language teachers adopt a blended learning approach that combines traditional classroom instruction with online and digital resources. This allows for a seamless integration of technology into language learning curricula.

Digital Language Portfolios, in which language teachers can implement digital language portfolios where students can showcase their language proficiency through multimedia elements. This includes audio recordings, videos, and digital projects.

Webinars and Online Language Events, in which language teachers organize webinars or virtual language events where students can interact with native speakers, language experts, or peers from different cultural backgrounds. This provides authentic language exposure and promotes global communication.

Gamification Platforms, in which language teachers can explore gamification platforms designed for language learning, incorporating elements of competition, rewards, and interactive challenges. Platforms like Kahoot! or Quizizz make language practice engaging and enjoyable.

Model Lesson Plan 1

PODCAST EXPLORATION

Objective: To enhance listening skills and promote authentic language use through podcast exploration.

The Procedure follows the steps below, in which teachers should:

1. Introduce the concept of podcasts and their role in real-life communication.
2. Curate a selection of podcasts in the target language, spanning different genres and topics.
3. Assign specific podcasts to individual students or small groups, and instruct them to listen actively.
4. After listening, facilitate group discussions where students share insights, vocabulary learned, and reflections on the content.
5. Encourage students to create their own short podcasts, summarizing key points or expressing opinions on a given topic.

CHAPTER III. FUNDAMENTALS OF COMMUNICATIVE LANGUAGE TEACHING

Model Lesson Plan 2

COLLABORATIVE GOOGLE DOCS WRITING

Objective: To foster collaborative writing skills using cloud-based technology.

The Procedure follows the steps below, in which teachers should:

1. Introduce collaborative writing using platforms like Google Docs, emphasizing its real-time collaboration features.
2. Assign a writing task, such as creating a collaborative story, dialogue, or essay, to be completed in groups.
3. Each group works on the document simultaneously, contributing ideas, editing, and providing feedback.
4. Facilitate a peer review session where groups exchange feedback on each other's collaborative writing.
5. Conclude with a class discussion on the benefits of collaborative writing and technology integration in language learning.

The integration of technology in Communicative Language Teaching represents a paradigm shift that aligns language education with the digital landscape of the 21st century. The theoretical foundations, practical strategies, and model lesson plans presented in this scientific exploration underscore the transformative potential of leveraging technology in language learning. As educators continue to refine their instructional approaches, the commitment to technology integration offers a pathway to creating dynamic, engaging, and technologically literate language learners.

Fundamental 12. Assessment Through Performance

Assessment through performance is a cornerstone of Communicative Language Teaching, emphasizing the evaluation of learners based on their ability to use language in real-life situations. Within this principle, assessment focuses on learners' ability to perform language tasks and demonstrate communicative competence rather than on rote memorization of grammar rules. By assessing through performance, CLT aims to shift the focus from rote memorization to the demonstration of practical language skills in authentic contexts.

Theoretical Foundations:

Performance-based assessment aligns with the principles of **Task-Based Language Teaching (TBLT)**, emphasizing the importance of language use in achieving communicative goals. Tasks are designed to assess learners' ability to apply language in meaningful situations. Furthermore, the concept of **authentic assessment** posits that evaluations should reflect real-world language use. Performance-based assessments mirror the authentic communication situations learners are likely to encounter outside the classroom.

Practical Applications:

The practical applications of this principle can be as follows:

Role-Playing and Simulations, in which language teachers incorporate role-playing and simulations as assessment tools. Tasks such as job interviews, travel scenarios, or customer service interactions allow learners to showcase their language proficiency in realistic contexts.

Project-Based Assessments, in which language teachers design assessments that involve project-based tasks, where learners collaborate to create presentations, reports, or multimedia projects. This assesses not only language skills but also teamwork and creativity.

Practical Implications:

Practical Implications can include:
- **Rubric Development**, in which language teachers should create detailed rubrics for performance-based assessments to provide clear

criteria for evaluation. This ensures transparency and helps learners understand the expectations.

- **Portfolio Assessment**, in which language teachers should implement portfolio assessment, where learners compile evidence of their language proficiency over time. Portfolios can include recordings, written samples, and project work that showcase a range of language skills.

- **Peer Assessment**, in which language teachers should incorporate peer assessment components into performance-based tasks. Peer evaluations not only provide additional perspectives but also promote a collaborative learning environment.

- **Feedback Sessions**, in which language teachers should prioritize feedback sessions following performance-based assessments. Constructive feedback guides learners in recognizing strengths and areas for improvement, facilitating continuous language development.

Model Lesson Plan 1

JOB INTERVIEW SIMULATION

Objective: To assess learners' ability to communicate effectively in a job interview scenario.

The Procedure follows the steps below, in which teachers should:

1. Introduce the concept of job interviews and the language typically used in such situations.
2. Provide a list of common interview questions and responses.
3. Assign roles to students, designating some as interviewers and others as job candidates.
4. Conduct simulated job interviews in pairs or small groups, with each student having an opportunity to play both roles.
5. Evaluate students based on their language use, clarity of communication, and appropriateness of responses.
6. Conclude with a feedback session where students reflect on their performance and receive constructive feedback.

Model Lesson Plan 2

Cultural Exchange Project Assessment

Objective: To assess learners' language proficiency through a collaborative cultural exchange project.

The Procedure follows the steps below, in which teachers should:

1. Divide the class into small groups, assigning each group a specific cultural theme or country.
2. Instruct groups to research and create a presentation that includes language use, cultural insights, and interactive elements.
3. Assess the presentations based on language accuracy, creativity, and the ability to engage the audience.
4. Encourage a Q&A session after each presentation, assessing students' ability to respond to questions in the target language.
5. Conclude with a reflective discussion on the value of performance-based assessments in showcasing language proficiency.

Assessment through performance stands as a powerful tool in the Communicative Language Teaching framework, emphasizing the practical application of language skills in authentic contexts. The theoretical foundations, practical applications, and model lesson plans presented in this scientific exploration underscore the transformative potential of performance-based assessment in language education. As educators continue to refine their assessment practices, a commitment to assessing through performance contributes to the development of communicatively competent and versatile language learners. This scientific inquiry adds depth to our understanding of the multifaceted dimensions of performance-based assessment within the CLT framework.

CHAPTER IV. CURRENT TRENDS IN COMMUNICATIVE LANGUAGE TEACHING

Since the 1990s, the communicative approach has been widely implemented. Because it describes a set of very general principles grounded in the notion of communicative competence as the goal of second and foreign language teach- ing, and a communicative syllabus and methodology as the way of achieving this goal, communicative language teaching has continued to evolve as our under- standing of the processes of second language learning has developed. Current communicative language teaching theory and practice thus draws on a number of different educational paradigms and traditions. And since it draws on a num- ber of diverse sources, there is no single or agreed upon set of practices that characterize current communicative language teaching. Rather, communicative language teaching today refers to a set of generally agreed upon principles that can be applied in different ways, depending on the teaching context, the age of the learners, their level, their learning goals, and so on.

Ten Core Assumptions in Modern CLT

The following core assumptions or variants of them underlie current practices in communicative language teaching:

1. Second language learning is facilitated when learners are engaged in interaction and meaningful communication.

2. Effective classroom learning tasks and exercises provide opportunities for students to negotiate meaning, expand their language resources, notice how language is used, and take part in meaningful interpersonal exchange.

3. Meaningful communication results from students processing content that is relevant, purposeful, interesting, and engaging.

4. Communication is a holistic process that often calls upon the use of several language skills or modalities.

5. Language learning is facilitated both by activities that involve inductive or discovery learning of underlying rules of language use and organization, as well as by those involving language analysis and reflection.

6. Language learning is a gradual process that involves creative use of language, and trial and error. Although errors are a normal product of learning, the ultimate goal of learning is to be able to use the new language both accurately and fluently.

7. Learners develop their own routes to language learning, progress at different rates, and have different needs and motivations for language learning.

8. Successful language learning involves the use of effective learning and communication strategies.

9. The role of the teacher in the language classroom is that of a facilitator, who creates a classroom climate conducive to language learning and provides opportunities for students to use and practice the language and to reflect on language use and language learning.

10. The classroom is a community where learners learn through collaboration and sharing.

Your turn:

What are the implications of the principles above for teaching in your teaching context? Do you have other principles that support your teaching?

_____
_____
_____
_____
_____
_____
_____
_____

Essential Characteristics of Traditional Classroom Activities

Current approaches to methodology draw on earlier traditions in communicative language teaching and continue to make reference to some extent to traditional approaches. Thus classroom activities typically have some of the following characteristics:

- They seek to develop students' communicative competence through linking grammatical development to the ability to communicate. Hence, grammar is not taught in isolation but often arises out of a communicative task, thus creating a need for specific items of grammar. Students might carry out a task and then reflect on some of the linguistic characteristics of their performance.

- They create the need for communication, interaction, and negotiation of meaning through the use of activities such as problem solving, information sharing, and role play.
- They provide opportunities for both inductive as well as deductive learning of grammar.
- They make use of content that connects to students' lives and interests.
- They allow students to personalize learning by applying what they have learned to their own lives.
- Classroom materials typically make use of authentic texts to create interest and to provide valid models of language.

Key Components of CLT in Today's World

Approaches to language teaching today seek to capture the rich view of language and language learning assumed by a communicative view of language. Jacobs and Farrell (2003) see the shift toward CLT as marking a paradigm shift in our thinking about teachers, learning, and teaching. They identify key components of this shift as follows:

1. Focusing greater attention on **the role of learners** rather than the external stimuli learners are receiving from their environment. Thus, the center of attention shifts from the teacher to the student. This shift is generally known as the move from teacher-centered instruction to learner-centered instruction.

2. Focusing greater attention on **the learning process** rather than the products that learners produce. This shift is known as the move from product-oriented to process-oriented instruction.

3. Focusing greater attention on **the social nature of learning** rather than on students as separate, decontextualized individuals

4. Focusing greater attention on **diversity among learners** and viewing these difference not as impediments to learning but as resources to be recognized, catered to, and appreciated. This shift is known as the study of individual differences.

5. In research and theory-building, focusing greater attention on the views of those **internal to the classroom** rather than solely valuing the views of those who come from outside to study classrooms, investigate and evaluate what goes on there, and engage in theorizing about it. This shift is associated

with such innovations as qualitative research, which highlights the subjective and affective, the participants' insider views, and the uniqueness of each context.

6. Along with this emphasis on context comes the idea of connecting the school with the world beyond as means of **promoting holistic learning**.

7. Helping students to understand **the purpose of learning** and develop their own purpose

8. **A whole-to-part orientation** instead of a part-to-whole approach. This involves such approaches as beginning with meaningful whole text and then helping students understand the various features that enable texts to function, e.g., the choice of words and the text's organizational structure.

9. An emphasis on **the importance of meaning** rather than drills and other forms of rote learning

10. A view of **learning as a lifelong process** rather than something done to prepare students for an exam.

Eight Major Changes in Approaches to Language Teaching

Jacobs and Farrell suggest that the CLT paradigm shift outlined above has led to eight major changes in approaches to language teaching. These changes are:

1. **Learner autonomy:** Giving learners greater choice over their own learning, both in terms of the content of learning as well as processes they might employ. The use of small groups is one example of this, as well as the use of self-assessment.

2. **The social nature of learning:** Learning is not an individual, private activity, but a social one that depends upon interaction with others. The movement known as cooperative learning reflects this viewpoint.

3. **Curricular integration:** The connection between different strands of the curriculum is emphasized, so that English is not seen as a stand-alone subject but is linked to other subjects in the curriculum. Text-based learning (see below) reflects this approach, and seeks to develop fluency in text types that can be used across the curriculum. Project work in language teaching also requires students to explore issues outside of the language classroom.

4. **Focus on meaning:** Meaning is viewed as the driving force of learning. Content-based teaching reflects this view and seeks to make the

exploration of meaning through content the core of language learning activities.

5. **Diversity:** Learners learn in different ways and have different strengths. Teaching needs to take these differences into account rather than try to force students into a single mold. In language teaching, this has led to an emphasis on developing students' use and awareness of learning strategies.

6. **Thinking skills:** Language should serve as a means of developing higher-order thinking skills, also known as critical and creative thinking. In language teaching, this means that students do not learn language for its own sake but in order to develop and apply their thinking skills in situations that go beyond the language classroom.

7. **Alternative assessment:** New forms of assessment are needed to replace traditional multiple-choice and other items that test lower-order skills. Multiple forms of assessment (e.g., observation, interviews, journals, portfolios) can be used to build a comprehensive picture of what students can do in a second language.

8. **Teachers as co-learners:** The teacher is viewed as a facilitator who is constantly trying out different alternatives, i.e., learning through doing. In language teaching, this has led to an interest in action research and other forms of classroom investigation.

These changes in thinking have not led to the development of a single model of CLT that can be applied in all settings. Rather, a number of different language teaching approaches have emerged which reflect different responses to the issues identified above. While there is no single syllabus model that has been universally accepted, a language syllabus today needs to include systematic coverage of the many different components of communicative competence, including **language skills**, **content**, **grammar**, **vocabulary**, and **functions**.

Different syllabus types within a communicative orientation to language teaching employ different routes to developing communicative competence. We will now examine some of the different approaches that are currently in use around the world and which can be viewed as falling within the general framework of communicative language teaching.

Your turn:

How can the eight changes discussed by Farrell and Jacobs influence language teaching practices in your school or district? Try them out and then write your experience below.

CHAPTER V. CLASSROOM ACTIVITIES IN CLT

Since the advent of CLT, teachers and materials writers have sought to find ways of developing classroom activities that reflect the principles of a communicative methodology. This quest has continued to the present, as we shall see later in the booklet. The principles on which the first generation of CLT materials are still relevant to language teaching today, so in this chapter we will briefly review the main activity types that were one of the outcomes of CLT.

Fluency & Accuracy Practices

One of the goals of CLT is to develop **fluency** in language use. Fluency is natural language use occurring when a speaker engages in meaningful interaction and maintains comprehensible and ongoing communication despite limitations in his or her communicative competence. Fluency is developed by creating classroom activities in which students must negotiate meaning, use communication strategies, correct misunderstandings, and work to avoid communication breakdowns.

Fluency practice can be contrasted with **accuracy practice**, which focuses on creating correct examples of language use. Differences between activities that focus on fluency and those that focus on accuracy can be summarized as follows:

Activities focusing on fluency
- Reflect natural use of language
- Focus on achieving communication
- Require meaningful use of language
- Require the use of communication strategies
- Produce language that may not be predictable
- Seek to link language use to context
Activities focusing on accuracy
- Reflect classroom use of language
- Focus on the formation of correct examples of language
- Practice language out of context
- Practice small samples of language
- Do not require meaningful communication

> - Control choice of language

Your turn:
Can you give examples of fluency and accuracy activities that you use in your teaching?

_____
_____
_____
_____
_____
_____
_____

The following are examples of fluency activities and accuracy activities. Both make use of group work, reminding us that group work is not necessarily a fluency task (Brumfit 1984).

Fluency Tasks

A group of students of mixed language ability carry out a role play in which they have to adopt specified roles and personalities provided for them on cue cards. These roles involve the drivers, witnesses, and the police at a collision between two cars. The language is entirely improvised by the students, though they are heavily constrained by the specified situation and characters.

The teacher and a student act out a dialog in which a customer returns a faulty object she has purchased to a department store. The clerk asks what the problem is and promises to get a refund for the customer or to replace the item. In groups, students now try to recreate the dialog using language items of their choice. They are asked to recreate what happened preserving the meaning but not necessarily the exact language. They later act out their dialogs in front of the class.

Accuracy Tasks

Students are practicing dialogs. The dialogs contain examples of falling intonation in Wh-questions. The class is organized in groups of three, two students practicing the dialog, and the third playing the role of monitor. The

CHAPTER V. CLASSROOM ACTIVITIES IN CLT

monitor checks that the others are using the correct intonation pattern and corrects them where necessary.

The students rotate their roles between those reading the dialog and those monitoring. The teacher moves around listening to the groups and correcting their language where necessary.

Students in groups of three or four complete an exercise on a grammatical item, such as choosing between the past tense and the present perfect, an item which the teacher has previously presented and practiced as a whole class activity. Together students decide which grammatical form is correct and they complete the exercise. Groups take turns reading out their answers.

Teachers were recommended to use a balance of fluency activities and accuracy and to use accuracy activities to support fluency activities. Accuracy work could either come before or after fluency work. For example, based on students' performance on a fluency task, the teacher could assign accuracy work to deal with grammatical or pronunciation problems the teacher observed while students were carrying out the task. An issue that arises with fluency work, how- ever, is whether it develops fluency at the expense of accuracy. In doing fluency tasks, the focus is on getting meanings across using any available communicative resources. This often involves a heavy dependence on vocabulary and com- munication strategies, and there is little motivation to use accurate grammar or pronunciation. Fluency work thus requires extra attention on the part of the teacher in terms of preparing students for a fluency task, or follow-up activities that provide feedback on language use.

While dialogs, grammar, and pronunciation drills did not usually dis- appear from textbooks and classroom materials at this time, they now appeared as part of a sequence of activities that moved back and forth between accuracy activities and fluency activities. And the dynamics of classrooms also changed. Instead of a predomi- nance of teacher-fronted teaching, teachers were encouraged to make greater use of small-group work. Pair and group activities gave learners greater oppor- tunities to use the language and to develop fluency.

Mechanical, Meaningful, and Communicative Practice

Another useful distinction that some advocates of CLT proposed was the distinction between three different kinds of practice – **mechanical, meaningful, and communicative**.

Mechanical practice refers to a controlled practice activity which students can successfully carry out without necessarily understanding the language they are using. Examples of this kind of activity would be repetition drills and substitu- tion drills designed to practice use of particular grammatical or other items.

Meaningful practice refers to an activity where language control is still provided but where students are required to make meaningful choices when carrying out practice. For example, in order to practice the use of prepositions to describe locations of places, students might be given a street map with various buildings identified in different locations. They are also given a list of prepositions such as across from, on the corner of, near, on, next to. They then have to answer ques- tions such as *"Where is the book shop? Where is the café?"* etc. The practice is now meaningful because they have to respond according to the location of places on the map.

Communicative practice refers to activities where practice in using language within a real communicative context is the focus, where real information is exchanged, and where the language used is not totally predictable. For example, students might have to draw a map of their neighborhood and answer questions about the location of different places, such as the nearest bus stop, the nearest café, etc.

Exercise sequences in many CLT course books take students from mechanical, to meaningful, to communicative practice. The following exercise, for example, is found in Passages 2 (Richards and Sandy 1998).

CHAPTER V. CLASSROOM ACTIVITIES IN CLT

Sample Exercise from CLT Coursebook

Superlative adjectives
Superlative adjectives usually appear before the noun they modify.

The funniest person I know is my friend Bob.
The most caring individual in our school is the custodian.

They can also occur with the noun they modify

Of all the people in my family, my Aunt Ruth is **the kindest**.
Of all my professors, Dr. Lopez is **the most inspiring**.

Superlatives are often followed by relative clauses in the present perfect.

My cousin Anita is **the most generous** person **I've ever met**.
The closest friend **I've ever had** is someone I met in elementary school.

A Complete these sentences with your own information, and add more details. Then compare with a partner.
    1. One of the most inspiring people I've ever known is …
One of the most inspiring people I've ever known is my math teacher. She encourages students to think rather than just memorize formulas and rules.

    2. The most successful individual I know is …
    3. Of all the people I know …. is the least self-centered.
    4. The youngest person who I consider to be a hero is …
    5. The most moving speaker I have ever heard is …
    6. The most important role model I've ever had is …
    7. Of all the friends I've ever had …. is the most understanding.
    8. One of the bravest things I've eve done is …

B Use the superlative form of these adjectives to describe people you know. Write at least five sentences.
    brave   honest   interesting   smart   generous   inspiring   kind   witty

C Group work
Discuss the sentences your wrote in Exercises A and B. Ask each other follow-up questions.
    A. My next-door neighbor is the bravest person I've ever met.
    B. What did your neighbor do, exactly?
    A. She's a firefighter, and once she saved a child from a burning building …

If students read and practice aloud the sentences in the grammar box, this constitutes mechanical practice. Exercises A and B can be regarded as meaningful practice since students now complete the sentences with their own information. Exercise C is an example of communicative practice since it is an open-ended discussion activity.

Your turn:
Examine the activities in one unit of a course book. Can you find examples of activities that provide mechanical, meaningful, and communicative practice? What type of activities predominate?

_____
_____
_____
_____
_____
_____
_____
_____

The distinction between mechanical, meaningful, and communicative activities is similar to that given by Littlewood (1981), who groups activities into two kinds:

Pre-communicative activities	Communicative activities
Structural activities	Functional communication activities
Quasi-communicative activities	Social interactional activities

Functional communication activities require students to use their language resources to overcome an information gap or solve a problem (see below). Social interactional activities require the learner to pay attention to the context and the roles of the people involved, and to attend to such things as formal versus informal language.

Information-Gap Activities

An important aspect of communication in CLT is the notion of information gap. This refers to the fact that in real communication, people normally com- municate in order to get information they do not possess. This is known as an information gap. More authentic communication is likely to occur in the class- room if students go beyond practice of language forms for their own sake and use their linguistic and communicative resources in order to obtain information. In so doing, they will draw available vocabulary, grammar, and communication strategies to complete a task. The following exercises make use of the informa- tion-gap principle:

Students are divided into A-B pairs. The teacher has copied two sets of pictures. One set (for A students) contains a picture of a group of people. The other set (for B students) contains a similar picture but it contains a number of slight differences from the A-picture. Students must sit back to back and ask questions to try to find out how many differences there are between the two pictures.

Students practice a role play in pairs. One student is given the information she/he needs to play the part of a clerk in the railway station information booth and has information on train departures, prices, etc. The other needs to obtain information on departure times, prices, etc. They role-play the interaction without looking at each other's cue cards.

Jigsaw activities

These are also based on the information-gap principle. Typically, the class is divided into groups and each group has part of the information needed to com- plete an activity. The class must fit the pieces together to complete the whole. In so doing, they must use their language resources to communicate meaning- fully and so take part in meaningful communication practice. The following are examples of jigsaw activities:

The teacher plays a recording in which three people with different points of view discuss their opinions on a topic of interest. The teacher prepares three different listening tasks, one focusing on each of the three speaker's points of view. Students are divided into three groups and each group listens and takes notes on one of the three speaker's opinions. Students are then rearranged into groups containing a student from groups A, B, and C. They now role-play the discussion using the information they obtained.

The teacher takes a narrative and divides it into twenty sections (or as many sections as there are students in the class). Each student gets one section of the story. Students must then move around the class, and by listening to each section read aloud, decide where in the story their section belongs. Eventually the students have to put the entire story together in the correct sequence.

Other Activity Types in CLT

Many other activity types have been used in CLT, including the following:

Task-completion activities

- puzzles,
- games,
- map-reading,
- and other kinds of classroom tasks in which the focus is on using one's language resources to complete a task.

Information-gathering activities

- student-conducted surveys,
- interviews,
- and searches in which students are required to use their linguistic resources to col- lect information.

Opinion-sharing activities

Activities in which students compare values, opinions, or beliefs, such as a ranking task in which students list six qualities in order of importance that they might consider in choosing a date or spouse.

Information-transfer activities

These require learners to take information that is presented in one form, and represent it in a different form. For example, they may read instructions on how to get from A to B, and then draw a map showing the sequence, or they may read information about a subject and then represent it as a graph.

Reasoning-gap activities

These involve deriving some new information from given information through the process of inference, practical reasoning, etc. For example, working out a teacher's timetable on the basis of given class timetables.

Role plays

Activities in which students are assigned roles and improvise a scene or exchange based on given information or clues. These activities incorporate role-playing scenarios to allow students to practice language in different social contexts, and help develop their speaking and listening skills in a more interactive way.

CHAPTER V. CLASSROOM ACTIVITIES IN CLT

Language Games

Games like word associations, bingo, or charades can reinforce vocabulary and language structures. Moreover, teacher can use language games to make learning more enjoyable and engaging.

Problem-Solving Activities:

This promotes critical thinking skills in addition to language development, integrating language learning with problem-solving activities that require communication to find solutions.

Emphasis on Pair and Group Work

Most of the activities discussed above reflect an important aspect of classroom tasks in CLT, namely that they are designed to be carried out in pairs or small groups. Through completing activities in this way, it is argued, learners will obtain several benefits:

- They can learn from hearing the language used by other members of the group.
- They will produce a greater amount of language than they would use in teacher-fronted activities.
- Their motivational level is likely to increase.
- They will have the chance to develop fluency.

Teaching and classroom materials today consequently make use of a wide variety of small-group activities.

Your turn:

What are some advantages and limitations of pair and group work in the language classroom?

Pair Work

Advantages	***Limitations***

Group Work

Advantages	Limitations
_____	_____
_____	_____
_____	_____
_____	_____
_____	_____
_____	_____
_____	_____

The Push for Authenticity

Since the language classroom is intended as a preparation for survival in the real world and since real communication is a defining characteristic of CLT, an issue which soon emerged was the relationship between classroom activities and real life. Some argued that classroom activities should as far as possible mirror the real world and use real world or "authentic" sources as the basis for classroom learning. Clarke and Silberstein (1977, 51) thus argued:

Classroom activities should parallel the "real world" as closely as possible. Since language is a tool of communication, methods and materials should concentrate on the message and not the medium. The purposes of reading should be the same in class as they are in real life.

Arguments in favor of the use of authentic materials include:
- They provide cultural information about the target language.
- They provide exposure to real language.
- They relate more closely to learners' needs.
- They support a more creative approach to teaching.

Others (e.g., Widdowson 1987) argued that it is not important if classroom materials themselves are derived from authentic texts and other forms of input, as long as the learning processes they facilitated were authentic. Critics of the case for authentic materials point out that:

- Created materials can also be motivating for learners.
- Created materials may be superior to authentic materials because they are generally built around a graded syllabus.

CHAPTER V. CLASSROOM ACTIVITIES IN CLT

- Authentic materials often contain difficult and irrelevant language.
- Using authentic materials is a burden for teachers.

However, since the advent of CLT, textbooks and other teaching materials have taken on a much more "authentic" look; reading passages are designed to look like magazine articles (if they are not in fact adapted from magazine articles) and textbooks are designed to a similar standard of production as real world sources such as popular magazines.

Your last turn:
How useful do you think authentic materials are in the classroom? What difficulties arise in using authentic materials?

Conclusion

In the journey through "CLT: Origins, Fundamentals, and Current Trends," we have embarked on a comprehensive exploration of Communicative Language Teaching (CLT), unraveling its historical roots, fundamental principles, and dynamic evolution in the contemporary landscape of language education. As we conclude this manual, let us reflect on the key insights gained and the transformative potential that CLT holds for educators, learners, and language enthusiasts alike.

The theoretical foundations of CLT provide a solid framework upon which the methodology is built. Concepts such as communicative competence, socio-cultural theories, and task-based language teaching serve as guiding beacons, illustrating the theoretical underpinnings that have shaped CLT since its inception. Understanding these foundations not only enriches our pedagogical knowledge but also underscores the rationale behind the fundamental principles of CLT.

The fundamentals of CLT, ranging from communication as the goal to the integration of technology, highlight the learner-centric approach that defines this methodology. By prioritizing authentic communication, focusing on language functions over structures, and embracing cultural sensitivity, CLT offers a holistic and dynamic language learning experience. Model lesson plans and practical examples further bridge the gap between theory and application, providing educators and learners with tangible strategies for effective implementation.

In the contemporary educational landscape, CLT continues to evolve, adapting to the challenges and opportunities presented by the digital age. The exploration of current trends within CLT, such as the use of technology, performance-based assessment, and cultural sensitivity, positions this manual as a guide to navigating the ever-changing terrain of language education. The integration of technology, in particular, has opened new avenues for interactive communication, expanding the possibilities for authentic language use and cultural exploration.

As we conclude this manual, let it serve as a testament to the enduring significance of CLT in shaping meaningful language learning experiences. Whether you are an educator seeking to refine your instructional strategies, a

Conclusion

learner navigating the intricacies of language acquisition, or a language enthusiast curious about the evolution of language teaching methodologies, "CLT: Origins, Fundamentals, and Current Trends" invites you to embrace the transformative potential of Communicative Language Teaching.

May this manual be a source of inspiration, innovation, and empowerment as you embark on the journey of fostering communicatively competent and culturally aware language learners. With the insights gained from this exploration of CLT, let us continue to shape the future of language education, where effective communication, cultural understanding, and dynamic language proficiency converge in a rich tapestry of linguistic excellence.

References:

1. Jalolov, J. J., Makhkamova G.T., Ashurov Sh. S. (2015) English language Teaching Methodology. Tashkent.
2. Auerbach, E. R. (1986). Competency-Based ESL: One Step Forward or Two Steps Back? TESOL Quarterly, 20 (3).
3. Beglar, David, and Alan Hunt (2002). Implementing task-based language teaching. In Jack Richards and Willy Renandya (eds). Methodology in Language Teaching: An Anthology of Current Practice. New York: Cambridge University Press.
4. Brown, H. Douglas (1994). Principles of Language Learning and Teaching.
5. Brown, J. D. (2005) Testing in Language Programs: A Comprehensive Guide to English Language Assessment
6. Brumfit, Christopher (1984). Communicative Methodology in Language Teaching. Cambridge: Cambridge University Press.
7. Canale and Swain. (1980) Theoretical Bases of Communicative Approaches to Second Language Teaching and Testing
8. Celce-Murcia, M. (2001). Teaching English as a Second or Foreign Language
9. Clarke, M., and S. Silberstein (1977). Toward a realization of psycholinguistic principles in the ESL reading class. Language Learning, 27 (1), 48–65.
10. Feez, S., and H. Joyce (1998). Text-Based Syllabus Design. Australia: Macquarie University
11. Holliday, A. (1999). Intercultural Communication and Ideology
12. Jacobs, G. M, & Farrell, T. S. C. (2003). Understanding and implementing the CLT (Communicative Language Teaching) paradigm. RELC Journal, 34(1), 5-30.
13. Krahnke, K. (1987). Approaches to Syllabus design for Foreign Language Teaching. Washington, DC: Center for Applied Linguistics.
14. Krashen, S. (1981). Second Language Acquisition and Second Language Learning
15. Levy, M. (1997). CALL Dimensions: Options and Issues in Computer-Assisted Language Learning
16. Littlejohn, A., and D. Hicks (1996). Cambridge English for Schools. Cambridge: Cambridge University Press.

Conclusion

17. Littlewood, W. (1981). Communicative Language Teaching. New York: Cambridge University Press.
18. Long, M. H. (2015) Second Language Acquisition and Task-Based Language Teaching
19. Mercer, N. (2000). Words and Minds: How We Use Language to Think Together
20. Nunan, D. (1989). Designing Tasks for the Communicative Classroom
21. Prabhu, N. S. (1987). Second Language Pedagogy. Oxford: Oxford University Press.
22. Richards, Jack C., and Theodore Rodgers (2001). Approaches and Methods in Language Teaching. Second Edition. New York: Cambridge University Press.
23. Richards, Jack C., and Charles Sandy (1998). Passages. New York: Cambridge University Press.
24. Rivers, W. M. (1981). Speaking in Many Tongues: Essays in Foreign-Language Teaching
25. Skehan, P. (1996). Second language acquisition research and task-based instruction. In J. Willis and D. Willis (eds). Challenge and Change in Language Teaching. Oxford: Heinemann.
26. Van Ek, J., and L. G. Alexander (1980). Threshold Level English. Oxford: Pergamon.
27. Widdowson. H. (1987). Aspects of syllabus design. In M. Tickoo (ed). Language Syllabuses: State of the Art. Singapore: Regional Language Centre.
28. Willis, Jane (1996). A Framework for Task-Based Learning. Harlow: Longman.

www.ingramcontent.com/pod-product-compliance
Lightning Source LLC
LaVergne TN
LVHW080354070526
838199LV00059B/3809